Tea,
hee, hee
JOKE
BOOK

TEA, HEE, HEE JOKE BOOK

Copyright © 2011 by Catherine and Theresa Rubino

All rights reserved. No portion of this book may be used or reproduced in any manner whatsoever -- mechanically, electronically, or by any other means including photocopying-- without written permission of the authors and publisher, TheSnooze.com.

Library of Congress Cataloging-in-Publication Data TBD

Tea, Hee, Hee Joke Book / jokes written by Catherine and Theresa Rubino

ISBN 978-0-9831768-2-4

1. Wit and humor, Juvenile 2. Riddles, Juvenile [1. Jokes, 2 Wit and humor]

I. Rubino, Catherine II. Rubino, Theresa

PRINT EDITION

10 9 8 7 6 5 4 3 2 1

Cover and Interior Design, Type setting, Printing and Binding: Catherine Rubino

Copy editing: Theresa Rubino

TheSnooze.com books are available at special discounts when purchased in bulk for premiums and sales promotions as well as for fund raising or educational use. Special editions or book excerpts can also be created to specification. For details, contact the authors at the address below.

www.catree.com

FINE PRINT: This book was written in the USA, on paper made in the USA, printed in the USA, using glue made in the USA, in the basement built in the USA. Both authors born in the USA, reside in the USA, work in the USA.

First printing September 2010 under title "Coffee, Tea, Hee Hee" HANDMADE LIMITED EDITION ("Coffee, Tea, Hee Hee" was split into two books: "Cuppa Jo'kes" and "Tea Hee Hee")

####

Thank You

This Book is dedicated to all of the original participants of TheSnooze.com Tea Joke Contest. Thank you for taking the time to write jokes with us.

The winners of the highly acclaimed
Tea Joke Contest at TheSnooze.com were:

Why was the lady cow teapot late to the party?
Because she was decaffeinated.
--Holly Douglas (winner of pignoli nuts)

How long does it take to ship tea from China by slow boat?
Oolong Time.
--Mensch Freborg (winner of pignoli nuts)

What is baby teapot's favorite game?
Peekoe-boo.
--Tea Risa (winner of chocolate covered almonds)

Backward

About fifteen years ago Theresa and I ran a much acclaimed joke contest at TheSnooze.com website. It was usually around the theme of food; hamburger jokes, ethnic food and so on. Each month we wrote new jokes and asked our loyal readers to contribute as well. We published the jokes online and sent prizes of pignoli nuts and chocolate covered almonds to the winners. Over the years as the internet grew, however, we noticed something else. Websites from various places were linking to our Tea Jokes contest page. Some were even taking our jokes and publishing them on their own websites. Some sites gave us credit, some did not. So instead of getting upset that other people wanted our jokes, we decided to compile them into this handy book. Now anyone who wants to read our Tea Jokes can do so here. We hope you enjoy reading this as much as we enjoyed writing it.

Sincerely,

Catherine Rubino

Forward

About fifteen years ago Theresa and I ran a much acclaimed joke contest at TheSnooze. com web site. It was usually around the theme of food; hamburger jokes, ethnic food and so on. Each month we wrote new jokes and asked our loyal readers to contribute as well. We published the jokes online and sent prizes of pignoli nuts and chocolate covered almonds to the winners. Over the years as the internet grew, however, we noticed something else. Web sites from various places were linking to our Tea Jokes contest page. Some were even taking our jokes and publishing them on their own web sites. Some sites gave us credit, some did not. So instead of getting upset that other people wanted our jokes, we decided to compile them into this handy book. Now anyone who wants to read our Tea Jokes can do so here. We hope you enjoy reading this as much as we enjoyed writing it.

Sincerely,

Catherine Rubino

Tea Jokes

What's a teapot's favorite dog?
Maltese.

Why did the teapot's lid rattle?
Because it was faulty.

Why did the teapot use a walker?
Because of his frailty.

What was the tap dance music in the tea cup's recital?
Tea for Two.

Why does lady teapot make short, sharp popping noises from her bottom?
Because she is farty.

What did the tea bag say to the pretzel?
You're salty.

What does the Buddhist tea hope to attain?
Teavana.

Who was the most nominated tea bag at the Oscars?
Meryl Steep.

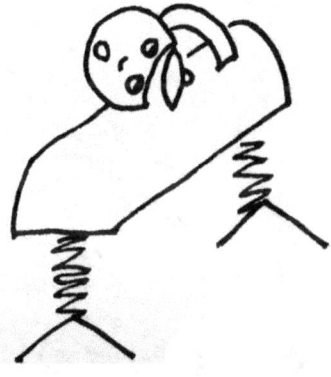

What's a tea bag's favorite Olympic event?
The Vaul-tea.

Who's the host on Deal or No Deal?
How-tea Mandel.

What did they say about the free-spirited tea bag?
She's tea loose and fancy free.

Who was that freckled marionette on TV with Buffalo Bob in the 50's?

How-tea doo-tea.

Where did the teapot get its Botox?

In its Liptons.

What does the tea say to the mouth wash?

You're minty.

What's a teapot's favorite movie snack?

Kettle corn.

What's a teapot's favorite game show?
Jeopar-tea.

What's a loose tea's favorite lullaby?
Rockaby baggy.

What is a teapot's favorite piece of culinary equipment?
A teaspoon.

What happened in the tea aisle during an earthquake?
It was calamity.

What's a teapot's favorite 70's show?
Teas Company.

What's a teapot's favorite 80's TV show character?
Tootie from Facts of Life.

Where do teapot's get all of their information?
Wiki-tea-dia.

What type of show did the teapot pitch to Hollywood?
Reali-tea?
No. A Steep-com.

Why did Earl Gray wear a crown?
Because he was royalty.

What's a teapot's favorite electronic device?
Tivo.

What Saint does Lady Teapot pray to?
St. Tea-resa.

What did daddy teapot get for his birthday?
Box Earls.

Why do the British like tea?
Because if they liked you they'd be too friendly.

Where do college age teapots buy their furniture?
I-TEA-A.

Why was lady teapot loaded with sugar?
Because she was a sweetie.

What is Earl Gray's favorite book?
War and Teas.

What is the tea bag's favorite 70's band?
Captain and Tea Neil.

And his favorite song?
Love Will Steep Us Together.

Why did the teapot paint its toenails?
For Vanity.

Why did old Mac Donald plant coffee bushes on his farm?
Because he's now selling coffee.

How many leaves does it take to make a tea bag?
Forty.

What did the tea get at the hospital?
An infusion.

Why do so many people drink tea?
Because they're thirsty.

What movie goes well with tea?
Monty Pie-thon.

Why did the tea cup blush?
Because it was Chai.

What shampoo does a teapot use?
Pantene.

Why did the teapot wear a jacket?
Because it wanted to be a person.

Why does tea like graham crackers?
Because they're crunch-tea.

Why do people put honey in tea?
Because they're sweeties.

Why did the white tea get passed over for the job?
Because of reverse dis-tea-mination.

What Beetle's song did teapot sing?
Let It Tea.

What candle did Mr. And Mrs. Teapot light at their wedding?
Unity.

What does a teapot say to its lover?
Oh darjeeling.

What did the secretary teapot say?
Coffee, Tea, Tea?

Why do people put tea cups on saucers?
To keep them from flying into outer space.

What movie inspired saucer to explore outer space?
Apollo Thirteen.

Why did the teapot go to the moon?
To live without gravity.

What did the American coffee mug say to the British Tea cup?
My you're dainty.

What was the teapot invited to?
A party.

Who is the teapot's favorite actress?
Tea Leoni.

Where does a teapot get its hair done?
At the Ceylon.

What does a teapot say to her hairdresser?
Don't tease.

Why did the tea bag have to do its laundry?
Because it was stained.

What does the teapot say to its bag?
I don't want another steep out of you.

What kind of music do teapots like?
Jasmine.

Why did the teapot wear a cosy?
Cos' he kept him warm.

What does a tea bag do when it's tired?
It steeps.

What does a lady teapot like to wear?
String of Earls.

What does a box of tea do when it moves to LA?
It has its bags tucked.

What's a teapot's favorite folk tune?
My Darjeeling Clementine.

Why did the teapot get in trouble?
Because he was naughty.

What did the teapot wear to bed?
A nighty.

Why did the tea get away?
Because it was loose.

Where do tea cups go when they die?
Eternity.

What does baby teapot wear?
Plastic panties.

What's the teapot's favorite Spielberg movie?
E.T.

What does mama teapot say to her little ones?
Don't spout off.

What bag did the elderly teapot wear on his side after his surgery?
His colos-tea-me.

Who is the tea bag's favorite rapper?
Ice-Tea.

Who's a teapot's favorite game show host?
Alex Tea-beck.

Why did the tea bag travel with an entourage?
Because it was a celebrity.

What does the baby teapot drink his tea out of?
His sip-tea cup.

What is the teapot's favorite Dickens' novel?
A Tale of Two Cities.

What is the tea cup's favorite love song lyric?
They're writing songs of love but not for tea.

What is a tea bag's favorite instrument?
The Tea-mpani.

Who is the tea bag's favorite Rapper?
Ice-T.

What is the teapot's favorite Disney character?
Mrs. Potts. That's too obvious.
Ok, Chip. Even so.
Tea-miny Cricket.

What do tea bags do when they go to sleep?
They tea-spoon.

What is Tony the Tiger's favorite cereal?
Fros-tea-d Flakes.

What flavor is Steve Jobs' favorite tea?
Apple.

What is the teapot's favorite musical?
My Fair La-Tea.

What is Donald Trump's favorite TV Show?
The Appren-teas.

Who is the tea bag's favorite actor?
Al Pa-tea-no.

Who is the tea bag's favorite director?
Quentin Taran-tea-no.

Who is the tea bag's favorite jazz pianist?
Oscar Tea-terson.

What did the boy tea bag say to the girl tea bag?
I think you're pu-erh tea.

What did the tea bag say when it got annoyed?
Leave me alone.

What is the tea bag's favorite movie?
Thelma and Loose Teas.

What is the tea bag's favorite time in history?
Tea Day and the Battle of Norman-Tea.

What did the mother tea bag say to her baby?
Time to go to steep.

What is the baby tea bag's favorite lullaby?
Rock-a-bye baggy.

What do you call a teapot that makes its own cosy?
Crafty.

What Tolstoy novel did mama teapot read several times?
Anna Karen-tea-na.

What Gustav Flaubert novel made sister teapot cry?
Madame Bover-tea.

What Anne Morrow Lindbergh book does mama teapot like?
Gift from the Tea.

Which Italian journalist does teapot read?
Oriana Fallac-tea.

What flower does teapot plant in her garden?
Tea-o-nese.

Who teaches at the tea cup school?
The Faculty.

What does a teapot take to the gym?
A tea bag.

How did the tea cup feel when the tea was gone?
Empty.

Why did the tea cup run from its critics?
Too much hostility.

Why did the teapot invite neighbors to dinner?
She believes in good hospitality.

What's a tea bag's favorite color?
Teal.

What's a tea cup's favorite letter?
T.

How does a baby learn about tea?
One steep at a time.

What is a teapot's favorite dance step?
The Chai Chai.

What's little tea cup's favorite ride?
The teeter totter.

Where do tea cups go for rest and relaxation?
St. Martinique.

Why was the box of tea up in the hay loft?
He was lofty.

What do little tea cups sing in the Christmas pageant?
Frosty the Snowman.

If a teapot had a hundred dollars what would it do with it?
Inves-tea-it.

What does little teapot play at summer camp?
T-ball.

What does daddy teapot invest in?
T-bills.

Where do teapots go on Saturday night?
The tea-ater.

Where do teapot's buy cheap goods?
Tea-wan.

What kind of jeans does a tea cup wear?
Gloria.

Why does a tea cup keep a journal?
Because it likes writing.

What do tea cups drink at happy hour?
Martini's.

What's warm, dark and made of leather?
A tee pee.

Where did the teapot do humanitarian work after an earthquake?
Haiti.

How does a tea cup get in the cookie jar?
On it's flying saucer.

Why is a teacup made of China?
Because it can't be made of Italy.

What Elton John song does teapot sing after work?
Don't Let the Sun Go Down on Tea.

What Bette Midler song did tea cup sing to its mom?
The Wind Beneath My Tea.

Badoom chink.

seep.

seep.

No guarantee on hilarity.

The End

hee hee

www.ingramcontent.com/pod-product-compliance
Lightning Source LLC
Chambersburg PA
CBHW050608300426
44112CB00013B/2126